THE AMAZING WORLD
of
LIVING THINGS

CONTENTS

Frontispiece: Britsh Kingfisher (page 71)

Chapter One
MAMMALS

Mammals are animals which feed their new-born offspring with the milk that is secreted from their bodies. Milk is the natural food for new-born mammals.

Humans, the most intelligent of all animals, are mammals. Mammals have hair on their bodies. It keeps them warm in the temperatures where they live. Humans, of course, do not have fur on their bodies like bears, nor wool like sheep but humans are able to make warm clothes to wear. The whale and the hippopotamus have very few hairs on their bodies.

POLAR BEARS

Polar bears have white fur and all other bears are either black or brown.

Polar bears have hair on the soles of their feet which gives them a good grip on the ice and snow of the north polar region where they live. They are very strong swimmers and in winter, they kill and eat seals and walruses as well as fish. Strangely, in the summertime, they eat a vegetable diet.

During the summer female polar bears build up their stores of fat in preparation for the long winter. Then they use caves under the snow, or dig dens in which to hibernate (or sleep). There they will give birth, in winter, to one or two cubs. The mothers are very protective of their young, especially from the male polar bears which might kill and eat their cubs if hungry.

GRIZZLY BEARS

Grizzlies are very big and powerful brown bears. They can reach a length of 2.5 metres and weigh 360 kilogrammes. These bears live among the mountains and woods of North America. They get their name from the colour of their silvery or grizzled coats. They are very dangerous when angry and can kill a big bison with a single blow.

They can move swiftly over the ground and swim well but their eyesight is very poor. They rely on their keen sense of smell when seeking food.

Bears mostly eat berries, wild fruit and insects. They usually sleep during the day and search for food at night. They dislodge stones and tear open rotten tree-stumps to find the grubs and insects which live underneath. Sometimes they dig out ground squirrels and small rats to eat.

In autumn, bears find caves or dens in which to hibernate through the long, winter months when there is little food about. They live by feeding on the stores of fat they have built up during the summer.

In winter, the bear cubs are born. They are naked, blind and no bigger than small rabbits. They remain in the den until they have fur and can walk. The cubs remain with their mother throughout the summer.

Usually at a sign of danger, bears run away but a human approaching a grizzly threateningly will probably be attacked and killed. All bears are extremely dangerous when their young are in danger and will fight to the death to protect them.

Grizzlies are not inclined to climb trees, probably because they are so heavy that it needs sturdy trunks to take their weight.

RED FOXES

The red fox is part of the dog family. It is found throughout North America, Europe and much of Asia. Wherever it lives, the fox is plentiful and is a highly successful hunter of small animals.

The fox hunts at night, coming out of its underground den at twilight and returning at dawn. The fox prefers to pounce on its prey rather than to chase it. Its habit of night hunting and the frequency with which it hunts in forests allows it plenty of opportunity to sneak up on its prey. Rabbits are perhaps the largest natural prey a fox will tackle; most of its victims are mice, earthworms and insects.

A fox will kill as often as it can, even if it is not hungry. The fox buries surplus kills, to be dug up a day or two later when food is not so plentiful. Once a fox gets into a chicken coop it will kill all the birds. It is this habit which has made foxes so unpopular with farmers.

Without doubt, the common fox of Great Britain is cleverer than all the other wild animals put together. This is probably because it is the most hunted of all animals. Chased by huntsmen and their hounds, the fox has had to use many clever tricks simply to stay alive. Running back on its own scent to confuse the huntsmen's dogs, or racing through a flock of sheep so that its own scent may be lost, are only two tricks of this cunning animal.

It even looks intelligent with its bright, alert eyes, pointed ears, which pick up the faintest sound, and long, pointed nose. In fact, if it were not for its long muzzle and bushy tail, a fox would look very much like a dog. Its underground home is called an earth which may be a hollow tree stump, a hole in a rock - or another creature's burrow it has stolen.

FACT FILE - RED FOX

Foxes are now living in cities, preying on garden birds and robbing dustbins.

FENNEC FOXES

The different types of foxes are members of the dog family. Although they are very similar to dogs and wolves, foxes tend to have longer bodies, shorter legs and most have bushy tails.

Fennec foxes live in the Sahara Desert of northern Africa and the deserts of Arabia. Fennecs can be recognised easily by their large eyes and ears. The large ears are not only used to listen for the movement of their vegetarian prey when they hunt at night but also enable the Fennec foxes to keep cool in the hot desert temperatures during the day because it is through their large ears that they lose any excess body heat. Also, as a protection against the heat underfoot, they have hair on their pads.

Young Fennecs

ARCTIC FOXES

In the northern regions of the world live the Arctic foxes. They usually live near the seacoasts although Arctic foxes have been sighted on ice floes 32 kilometres from shore.

Single Arctic foxes have been known to roam for hundreds of kilometres to forests inland.

There are two kinds of Arctic foxes; the blue (above) which in summer is a dark blueish grey and in winter a light blueish grey, and the white type. This is white in winter and brown in summer. In areas where the winters are not severe, the white Arctic fox sometimes remains a dark colour all the year round.

They have long hairs on the soles of their feet and this helps to prevent them from slipping and sliding on the ice when they are in pursuit of prey. They are not very particular about what they eat. They will feed on dead whales or dead seals, on fish, squirrels, hares and any birds they are clever enough to catch.

Arctic foxes are as cunning as any other type of fox. For instance, they will keep watch on polar bears and wait for kills to be made. They will then eat whatever the bear leaves.

They dig burrows in which to live, usually in the side of a cliff or a hill. When icy winds are blowing or snowfalls are heavy, Arctic foxes take shelter in these burrows.

Female foxes give birth to their young in May or June and may bear as many as eleven cubs. The parents take care of their young until the autumn.

LIONS

The lion is known as King of the Jungle, but in fact lions prefer to live in groups called prides on the open plains where the animals on which they prey are to be found.

Lions are second only to tigers in size among the cats. A male lion will often be over 2.8 metres in length and some may reach 3.4 metres. Male lions are larger and more powerful than the lionesses, but they rarely hunt. Instead their role is to protect the kill from scavengers, such as hyenas. If a lion hunts on its own it may only succeed in making a kill once for every ten times it begins a hunt.

FACT FILE - LIONS

Lions used to live in southern Europe. They died out in Greece and Italy about 2,000 years ago.
In 1898 two lions attacked workers building the Kenya to Uganda Railway at Tsavo. They killed and ate twenty-eight workers and building had to be halted for weeks until the lions were shot.

Lions are the only big cats known to hunt in groups; all other cats hunt alone. Lionesses do most of the hunting. A favourite trick is for most of the lionesses to lie in ambush while a single lioness approaches the prey, of zebra or antelope, from the opposite direction.

As soon as the prey see the lone lioness they flee in the opposite direction, straight towards the waiting pride. Lions prefer to hunt large prey, such as zebra but, when game is scarce, they will hunt wild pigs and small antelope.

Because lions are highly successful hunters they do not need to spend all their time running down prey. Much of a lion's time is spent dozing in the shade, or resting in the branches of trees.

TIGERS

The tiger is the largest of all the cats. A large, male tiger may measure 3.1 metres in length, while a few animals will be over 3.6 metres long and weigh over 320 kilogrammes.

With such a size and bulk, the tiger is a formidable hunter, able to prey on almost any animal it encounters. Only the wild pig, equipped with sharp tusks, can defend itself successfully.

Tigers live alone, though the ranges of several tigers may overlap. When the population becomes overcrowded, tigers

Left: *An Indian tiger* **Below:** *A tiger stalking sambar in India.*

Above: *Two male tigers fight for territory.*

Right: *The face markings are different on each tiger.*

may fight for territory. Such fights are now much rarer because the tiger is less numerous than it once was. In recent years the forests and scrubland where the tiger loves to hunt have been cleared to provide farmland.

Tigers are hunted to provide ingredients for Chinese medicines. Tigers are rare in most areas and have vanished completely from many lands where they were once common.

There are several types of tigers. The largest is the Siberian tiger while the smallest is the Java tiger, which rarely measures over 2.5 metres. The Siberian is probably the rarest and may soon be extinct in the wild unless it is protected properly.

FACT FILE - TIGERS

Most tigers avoid humans, but a man-eater in India killed and ate four hundred and thirty-eight people before it was shot in 1911. Hungry tigers will eat insects if no other food is available.

Above: *A tiger avoids a charging wild pig.*

SPOTTED CATS

There are about thirty-five species of cats in the world. All are graceful and supple hunters which feed on a variety of prey, using their powerful teeth and claws.

Most common of the larger cats is the leopard (above). It lives throughout Africa and southern Asia. Leopards prefer to live in or near forests, though they hunt on grasslands. Leopards hunt at night and can kill so silently that nearby animals are undisturbed. Usually leopards prey on antelope, monkeys, birds and lizards, but they sometimes attack dogs. Rarely will a leopard attack humans. One man-eating leopard in India killed over four hundred people before it was shot in 1910 by the famous hunter, Colonel Jim Corbett.

The clouded leopard (left) is about half the size of the leopard shown above and lives in the forests of south-eastern Asia.

Above: *The cheetah, the fastest of all cats, can reach 96 kilometres per hour in short bursts.*

Below: *The snow leopard is a very rare animal of the Himalayas and nearby mountain ranges. It hunts goats and ibex in the high mountains.*

FACT FILE - SPOTTED CATS

Some leopards have entirely black fur and are called panthers.
Cheetahs became extinct in India in 1954, and are now threatened in Africa.

SMALL CATS

All cats, no matter what their size, belong to the family Felidae, part of the carnivora order. Like their larger cousins, the leopards and lions, the small cats display all the special characteristics of the cat family. They have flexible and muscular bodies together with supple and powerful limbs. All the smaller cats have claws which can be retracted to keep them sharp for hunting.

The lynx is a beautifully-marked cat from Europe, Asia and North America. Unlike most cats, the lynx has a short, stumpy tail and prominent tufts of hair on its ears. The lynx hunts at night, silently stalking the undergrowth of northern forests in search of rodents and other small mammals.

The attractive, spotted fur made that animal the quarry of fur trappers in the past. More recently, the animal has been protected in most areas, but its numbers are still dropping.

The European wildcat lives not only in Europe but also in parts of Africa and Asia. This cat is muscular and powerful for its size. It may be found in dense forests, open grasslands or in dry deserts.

The wildcat preys on almost anything it can catch and kill, but usually hunts birds and small mammals. Kittens are born in a nest built in a hollow tree or dug out of the ground. Until they are about five weeks old they are almost helpless, but then begin to learn how to survive and hunt for themselves. At five months the kittens are fully grown and live independent lives.

It is thought that the domestic cat was bred from the wildcat, though the Libyan cat may also have been its ancestor.

Nobody is certain why cats were domesticated. It may be that their ability to hunt rats and mice brought them together with humans with both cats and humans then benefiting from the association.

Over the centuries that cats have lived with humans, they have been carefully bred in order to produce different breeds. Some of these breeds are named after the areas where they were first created, such as the Abyssinian, Siamese, Persian and Siberian. Others are named from their appearance,

Abyssinian cat.

Siamese cat.

Siberian cat.

as is the brown, short-haired tabby. The majority of domestic cats do not belong to any particular breed, but are crossbred to produce the typical 'moggy'.

Facing page: *A European wildcat.*
Bottom: *A lynx.*

Above: *The head of a domestic tabby cat.*

Below: *The beautiful, long hair of a domestic Persian.*

FACT FILE - CATS

A few cats grow flaps of skin, like wings, on their backs and use these to glide when leaping from trees and buildings.

Brown, short-haired tabby.

DOGS

Dogs have been pets of humans for thousands of years. Nobody is quite certain when or why dogs first became domesticated. Perhaps dogs took food from prehistoric humans in return for warning of the approach of dangerous bears or lions. It is generally thought that domestic dogs are descended from wolves, but the jackal may be an ancestor. Or the dog may be a cross between the two animals.

Domestic dogs generally have long snouts with up to forty-four teeth in the jaws. The claws do not retract, like those of domestic cats, so the claws become blunt and stout. Unlike most wild dogs, the domestic dog eats quantities of biscuits and other non-meat food. When dogs run wild they will eat plant material as well as hunt animals.

Over the millennia that dogs have been

kept by humans, the original dog has been selectively bred to produce a wide range of different breeds. Each breed has different characteristics, depending on the task for which it was bred. It is thought that the oldest breed may be the bloodhound, bred to have a keen sense of smell to follow deer and other game through dense forests.

Above: *The Old English Sheepdog was trained to help control sheep and to warn of danger.*

Below: *The Spaniel was bred to retrieve gamebirds for hunters, especially in marshes.*

Above: *The St Bernard which became famous as a search dog used to locate travellers who became lost in the snows of the St Bernard Pass in the Alps.*

Below: *A Bull terrier, bred to fight bulls but now kept as a pet.*

FACT FILE - DOGS

Domestic dogs love their homes. Often if a dog is lost it will walk home on its own. In 1979 an Alsatian lost on holiday in Arizona walked over 2,000 miles to its home in Washington State, taking four months to complete the journey.

WILD DOGS

Wild dogs are animals which belong to the family Canidae, part of the large carnivora (meat-eating) group. They all have certain characteristics in common with each other and with domestic dogs. For instance their claws are fixed and cannot be pulled back into the foot. Claws, therefore, tend to be stout but blunt. They are also skilled runners and able to overtake most of their prey. Most dogs also have long and bushy tails.

The most widespread wild dog is probably the wolf which was originally found across Europe, northern Asia and North America. Because wolves attack cattle and sheep, humans have hunted them to extinction in most areas. Wolves live in packs of over a dozen individuals which work together when hunting prey.

The coyote grows to about a metre in length. It hunts lizards, snakes and small mammals.

The jackal hunts at night when it attacks sheep and goats if working in a pack, or preys on lizards and birds if hunting alone.

The spotted hyena belongs to the Hyaenid family, related to dogs and cats. It scavenges meat from dead animals, but will also hunt live prey.

Facing page: (top) *A timber wolf and* **(bottom)** *a coyote, both from North America.*
Above: *A spotted hyena from the plains and savannahs of Africa.*
Below: *A pair of jackals which live in North Africa, parts of south-eastern Europe and southern Asia.*

BADGERS

Above: *The striped face of the badger.*

Badgers are powerful hunters about a metre long. They live in forests and woodlands in many European countries.

They are not often seen during the daytime and emerge to hunt for food when darkness falls. They will scuttle swiftly out of sight should danger threaten.

Badgers are closely related to weasels and skunks but they do not have their acute sense of smell. They rest during daylight hours in a deep burrow known as a sett. This may have several rooms and extend for many metres. It will also have more than one entrance. Perhaps because the setts are in daily use as a family home from one year to another, badgers are extremely clean animals. They clear away the entrances to their burrows and renew their setts with fresh leaves and grass. They also continually remove unwanted matter from the setts.

FACT FILE - BADGERS

The largest known badger weighed over 27 kilogrammes.
Badgers can dig faster than rabbits, which they chase underground.

Below: *A badger sniffing for food.*

On their nightly hunts for food they may travel for several miles along paths their grandparents travelled many years earlier. They leave their setts about an hour after sunset to hunt for earthworms, mice, snails and other small creatures. Badgers are also fond of fruit and honey.

They have very sharp claws and powerful front legs with which to dig out their food or turn over chunks of rotting trees to find the grubs they enjoy.

The European badger remains active throughout the long winter months, unlike Russian badgers which hibernate. Litters of two to four baby badgers are born between February and April. Fed by their mother, they eat and sleep in their setts until they are old enough to venture forth.

There are several types of badgers in the world. The small hog badger lives in China as does the ferret badger which sometimes climbs trees to hunt for food. Honey badgers which live in Africa and southern Asia, are, like European badgers, very fond of honey.

They feel no pain from bees' stings for they have thick fur and tough hides.

When walking with friends through woodlands look for signs of a badger. Often there are plenty. Notable clues are the pawprints, scratch marks on a tree, or fur caught in barbed wire.

Above: *Young badgers sleep in the warm, clean sett.*
Below: *A mother badger removes old leaves and replaces them with fresh leaves and grass to make a new bed.*

Signs of a badger: Left: *Pawprints.* **Centre:** *Scratch marks on the trunk of a tree.* **Right:** *Fur caught in barbed wire.*

Kangaroos live only in Australia. They are marsupial mammals, which means that the mothers keep the young safe and sound in pouches for many weeks after birth. Kangaroos still in their mothers' pouches are called joeys.

There are nearly sixty different types of kangaroos, all of which have some features in common. All kangaroos have very long and powerful hind legs which are used for hopping. The long tail is used to balance the creature while it is hopping. Small species of kangaroos are usually called wallabies.

The majority of kangaroos live on the open plains of central Australia. They feed on grass and other vegetation. The daytime temperatures can reach over thirty degrees Celsius. Fortunately, kangaroos have bare forearms, which they lick to cool the blood.

KANGAROOS

Kangaroos often have to travel over vast distances to find food or water. Hopping is a relatively efficient method of movement and kangaroos can maintain a high speed for hours at a time.

Facing page: Top: *A female grey kangaroo with its joey in the pouch.* **Bottom:** *A pair of male grey kangaroos kick each other during a courtship fight.* **Below:** *A large red kangaroo with a pair of grey kangaroos.*

ANTEATERS

Right: *The giant armadillo which lives in South America. This creature has large claws to dig into termites' nests and is covered with protective, horny plates.*

Below: *The pangolin also has large claws with which it attacks ants' nests, but it lives in central Africa. It will roll up into a ball if attacked, relying on its scales to protect it.*

Many different mammals have evolved to feed on ants, termites and other insects. To be successful at this, these mammals have the ability to dig into ants' nests and collect the insects with their sticky tongues. Most animals of this type belong to the Edentate order, which means they have no front teeth or no teeth at all.

The aardvark lives in Africa and is active only at night. It uses its large ears to listen for insects in the dark. When it finds insects, it uses its long, sticky tongue to lick them up.

The tree anteater lives in the forests of South and Central America. It uses its muscular tail to keep hold of a branch while it uses its front legs to smash open insect nests. Although it climbs well, the tree anteater can move only clumsily on the ground.

The giant anteater lives in forests and on grasslands in South America. It can grow to be 2.1 metres long and usually lives alone. If attacked, it rears up on its hind legs and lashes out with its powerful front claws.

The long nosed spiny anteater of New Guinea usually weighs from 4 to 5 kilogrammes. It is now very rare.

The aardwolf is a type of hyena which has evolved to hunt termites at night. It has a long, sticky tongue to lick up the insects, but will also eat eggs and small mammals if it gets the chance.

LEMURS

Lemurs live only on Madagascar, a large island off the south-eastern coast of Africa. There are twenty-eight species of lemur.

Above: *The aye-aye uses its long fingers to probe into crevices as it hunts insects at night.*
Below: *The indri is the largest lemur, being about 75 centimetres long.*

The sifaka is found in the dense forests of western Madagascar. It usually lives in family groups of about a dozen animals. It easily finds food of fruit and leaves and spends most of the day sleeping on a tree's upper branches.

FACT FILE - LEMURS

Lemurs once lived in Africa, but are now extinct there.
Lemurs are related to monkeys, apes and humans.

The ring-tailed lemur is the best known species because it can be kept easily in zoos. It lives in the dry, hilly areas of southern Madagascar. It eats grass and fruit and drinks tree sap. The ring-tailed lemur lives in large groups of about forty animals which are ruled by the females. The males will sometimes move from one group to another, but females always stay together.

MONKEYS

Monkeys are primates, like apes and lemurs. There are about a hundred types of monkeys, which are divided into two main groups. The New World monkeys live in South America and have grasping tails. The Old World monkeys live in Africa and Asia and cannot use their tails to grip objects.

Uakaris (top left) are New World monkeys living in small groups in the Amazon rainforest on fruit and small animals. The woolly monkey (far left) is also a New World monkey of the Amazon rainforest. It lives high in the trees to find its food of fruit and leaves. It lives in groups of about sixty individuals.

The lion-tailed macaque (above) lives in India and is an Old World monkey. In the mangrove swamps of Borneo lives the proboscis monkey (left). The large nose of the male is probably used to amplify its loud cry. The female has a much smaller nose and a quieter call.

FACT FILE - MONKEYS

In the First World War the 3rd South African Infantry Regiment used a monkey named Jackie as a lookout. He was wounded in 1918 and given a medal.

GORILLAS

Gorillas are the largest of all the primates, the highest order of mammals including man. They can grow to be 1.7 metres tall and weigh 210 kilogrammes. They are immensely powerful creatures which are quite capable of tearing down tree branches. When a gorilla is disturbed it will rear on its hind legs and beat its chest while roaring in a terrifying manner. If the intruder does not depart the gorilla will charge, thrashing the vegetation and bellowing its rage. Most intruders are so terrified that they flee at once.

However, the gorilla is only rarely a dangerous animal. It much prefers to live quietly among the rainforests of western Africa where it feeds on fruit, leaves and leaf shoots.

Gorillas usually live in family groups which have a complex social system. The

each other with chest-beating and roars until one gives way. Gorillas sleep at night, and usually doze or rest during the hottest part of the day. They find all the food they need in the few hours after dawn and before dusk.

They make their homes on platforms of sticks and branches which they build daily in trees a few feet above the ground. Even so they spend much of their time on the ground and amble around on all fours, supporting themselves by the use of their long and powerful arms.

They seldom attempt to attack humans. They become very vicious only if they are frightened or trapped.

FACT FILE - GORILLAS

The largest gorilla ever known weighed 280 kilogrammes and stood 1.7 metres tall.
There are two types of gorillas. The lowland gorilla has a paler coat than the mountain gorilla.

group is led by an old male, who may be up to forty years old. There are usually two or three other adult males in the group together with perhaps ten females and several juveniles. The old male leads the group through the forest in the endless search for food.

Each group has its own territory through which they wander. The territory may cover up to 35 square kilometres and frequently overlaps with that of neighbouring groups. If two groups meet, the males will threaten

ORANG-UTANS

The orang-utan lives in the dense forests of Sumatra and Borneo. It uses its powerful arms and legs to clamber through the trees in search of fruit, seeds and sometimes eggs. Each night the orang-utan builds a nest of twigs high in a tree in which to sleep. It stands about 1.5 metres tall and, when erect, its hands reach its ankles.

CHIMPANZEES

Chimpanzees live in the forests and open woodlands of central Africa. They live in groups of up to thirty animals and have a complex social life. They are able to use tools and are generally thought to be the most intelligent of the apes.

Chimpanzees grow about 1.6 metres tall, with slender, but muscular, arms and legs. They spend the day searching for fruit, nuts and eggs as they move through their territory. Chimpanzees often make nests of branches and leaves in which to sleep at night.

BABOONS

Baboons are Old World monkeys which live mostly on the ground in Africa. There are several types of baboons.

The chacma baboon (above) is one of the most common. They grow to about a metre long and live in groups of up to a hundred animals. The group, when faced by danger, may drive off a leopard or lion.

They mainly eat plants but sometimes they will catch birds and lizards.

Chacma baboons are active in the morning and the late afternoon. When the sun is at its highest, they rest in the shade.

Groups of baboons are known as troops and are made up of an old male with several females and their young. When on the move, the females and young stay near the centre of the troop while the younger males surround them. If danger threatens, the males approach the threat allowing the females time to escape.

Baboons are not usually dangerous to man but, if a large group feels threatened, it may attack and kill a human intruder. In some areas of Africa, like several other animals, baboons have become a major pest. They raid orchards for fruit and kill lambs and calves for food.

SLOTHS

The two-toed sloth (with two toes on each foot) lives in the forests of northern South America. It is active only at night, when it clambers through the branches for fruit and leaves to eat. The three-toed sloth (with two toes on its front feet and three toes on its back feet) is smaller and lives across a wider area of South America. Both sloths move very slowly. It is thought that they can move no faster than about 0.15 kilometres per hour. However, they can lash out with their hooked claws if they are attacked. Their fur is covered with algae (microscopic plants), which make them look green.

BUSHBABIES

Bushbabies are members of the group of animals known as primates. This group includes humans, apes and monkeys. There are several different kinds of bushbabies. They are all lively, gentle, little creatures.

Bushbabies make delightful pets, for in captivity they seem to be happy and playful. The greater bushbaby grows to be 45 centimetres in length, and the tail can be as long again.

It lives in forests, open woodland and among orchards in almost every area of Africa south of the Sahara Desert.

A bushbaby sleeps during the daytime. It finds a place in a tree where it can make a nest of leaves (right). There it rests until dusk. The bushbaby then begins to move around the branches and from tree to tree. It eats insects, lizards, small birds and any eggs it can find.

With its keen, large eyes the bushbaby can see well and hunt in the faint starlight. Because its eyes are so large, they are unable to move in their sockets. This is why a bushbaby needs to move its whole head from side to side to look in different directions.

The lesser bushbaby is smaller than the greater bushbaby. It is only 18 centimetres long with a 20 centimetres tail. However, it leads a similar life, except that it eats fruit and seeds as well as small animals.

Both types of bushbabies have strong hands and feet and this allows them to leap through the trees at great speed and so noiselessly that they have little difficulty in catching the insects and the birds they need to eat.

SQUIRRELS

Squirrels are rodents, as are mice, with strong, gnawing teeth at the front of their mouths. There are about two hundred and fifty different types of squirrels. The only countries they do not inhabit are those of Australasia.

The red squirrels live in the forests of Europe and northern Asia. They eat mainly seeds from the pine cones of the fir trees which grow in the cooler, northern forests. Squirrels are very agile. They can scamper up tree trunks and leap from tree to tree. The females build a small nest, (called a drey) from twigs and moss in which to rear the young. Although they live alone, red squirrels will sometimes join a group of several hundred and set off on a migration lasting several weeks and covering over 500 kilometres. Nobody is certain why.

Grey squirrels live in the deciduous forests of eastern North America. They are slightly larger than red squirrels, but not so agile. The grey squirrels eat almost any type of seed, attack birds' nests for eggs and hunt insects. They will eat tree bark if no other food is available causing damage to trees.

During the winter, the grey squirrels sleep for several weeks if the weather is particularly cold. About a hundred years ago, grey squirrels were introduced into Britain. They have spread rapidly and are replacing the red squirrels in many areas.

RATS

There is hardly anything good one can say about rats. They harbour the fleas which carry plague. They eat every food that humans eat and inflict untold damage on rabbit and bird populations and any grain or cereal.

Brown rats (right) are believed to have originated in China. They gradually travelled all over the world with the aid of shipping. Likewise, black rats came from India in the thirteenth century. They were the cause of a terrible outbreak of bubonic plague known as the Black Death. It was carried by the fleas from the black rat. Often the infection spread from overseas as ships' rats made their way down mooring ropes when a vessel docked. At least a quarter of the population of Europe perished from the plague. Brown rats will fight and devour

their weaker cousins, the black rats, and will eat members of their own kind who are trapped or disabled. They produce several litters every year and there may be as many as fourteen baby rats in one litter.

FACT FILE - RATS

The teeth of a brown rat are so strong, it can gnaw through a lead pipe to reach water.

MICE

There are hundreds of different types of mice throughout the world. The main groups are Old World mice, living in Africa, Europe and Asia with about four hundred species, and the New World mice of the Americas with three hundred and fifty species. Mice are fairly small animals with strong, gnawing teeth. They eat many types of seed and fruit and are often thought of as pests by humans.

Harvest Mice

Dormice

Long-tailed Field Mouse

Striped Field Mouse

Pet White Mice

Garden Dormouse

Kangaroo Mouse

Spiny Mouse

Yellow-necked Mouse

House Mice

WHALES

Whales are the largest animals alive today. They are mammals which have evolved to live in the sea.

There are over seventy different types of whales, divided into two main groups. The toothed whales include the dolphins and porpoises as well as whales. The baleen whales feed by filtering plankton and other tiny sea creatures from the water using baleen, a type of special horny plate in the mouth. Whales have been hunted by humans for many years. In some countries, whale meat is a favourite food, but most whales are hunted for their fat and for special chemicals in their bodies. Many types of whale are now very rare and are protected against hunters by international law. Other whales are relatively common and are still hunted.

The bowhead whale (below) lives in the Arctic Ocean and is a species of baleen whale. It is very rare and is now protected against hunters.

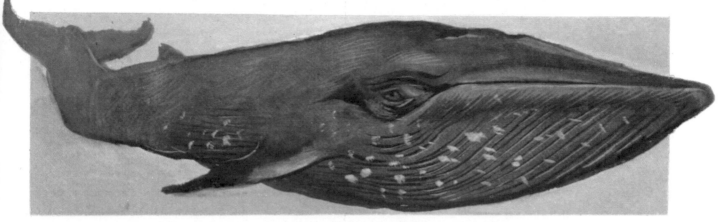

The baleen also called the blue whale is the world's largest animal. It may grow to 34 metres in length. It spends the winter in tropical waters and the summer near the Poles.

Above: *The killer whale, or orca, grows to 9.5 metres long. It hunts seals, fish and almost anything it can catch. Orcas hunt in packs, helping each other to kill prey.*

Below left: *The humpback whale is a baleen whale which is found in most oceans. It lives in groups of up to six animals and may grow to about 20 metres in length.*

Below right: *The sperm whale is the largest toothed whale. It hunts fish and squid and may dive to over 3,000 metres beneath the sea surface to hunt for food.*

SEALS

Seals are mammals which live in the sea. They have flippers instead of legs, and need to come to the surface to breathe.

Seals live all around the world. They spend most of their time in the water, where they hunt for fish and other animals. Seals are expert swimmers. They have streamlined bodies that slide easily through the water and flippers which provide power and help the seal to steer. Seals have a thick layer of fat beneath their skin. This keeps them warm and allows them to hunt in the cold waters near the North and South Poles.

During the summer seals come ashore. It is on beaches and rocky shores that female seals give birth to their young, called pups. In some species, pups are a beautiful white for the first few weeks of life. On land, seals move very slowly because their flippers are designed for swimming. Bears and other hunters, including man, can catch seals easily on land. Some types of seal are rare and are protected against hunters.

The grey seal lives in the northern Atlantic Ocean. It hunts fish and octopus near the coasts of Britain, Europe and Canada. It is about 2 metres in length.

FACT FILE - SEALS

The elephant seal is the world's largest seal at 6 metres in length. Crabeater seals do not eat crabs, they eat shrimps and prawns.

ELEPHANTs

tonnes. It lives in the open forests and grasslands of Africa, south of the Sahara. It eats leaves and fruits and will sometimes dig up roots for food.

Elephants usually live in herds governed by an old female. They help each other to find food and when in trouble. Sometimes a male will be excluded from the herd and will tear down trees and attack any animal it finds. These are called rogue elephants and they can be dangerous. The African elephant is a protected animal and is becoming more numerous.

The Indian elephant is now almost extinct in the wild. The forests where it lives have been cut down to provide farmland for the growing population of India. However, Indian elephants can be trained and are used to move heavy loads, such as tree trunks, in areas

Elephants are the world's largest, living land animals. There are two species, the African (above) and the Indian (right). Both these elephants are becoming rare. Their natural homes are being destroyed to create farmland and they are secretly hunted for their ivory tusks.

The African elephant is the larger of the two. It is often over 3 metres tall and weighs over 5

where there are no roads. Large numbers survive in captivity. They are often used in ceremonial parades.

Indian elephants live in India, Indo-China and Sumatra. They are nearly 3 metres tall but are smaller than African elephants. Their ears and tusks are smaller.

Both African and Indian elephants live for about sixty years. Although these animals are the biggest in the world, the remains of dead elephants are rarely found.

FACT FILE - ELEPHANTS

The largest elephant ever was a male African elephant which was shot in Namibia in 1978. It stood 4.3 metres tall and weighed 10 tonnes.

In 1928 an Indian elephant became rogue in the Blat Valley. It destroyed crops and killed several villagers. Sir George Maxwell, a famous hunter, decided to kill it. He travelled up the river, but on his first night the rogue ripped the boat from its moorings and overturned it. Sir George nearly drowned. It took several days for him to kill the rogue.

HORSES

The horse is one of man's oldest and best friends. Over fifty million years ago there lived an animal called the eohippus (left). It was one of the earliest ancestors of the horse we know today, although not much bigger than a fox. It had four toes on its front feet and three on its hind feet. It had a short and insignificant tail.

Millions of years later the unbounded swamplands where the eohippus lived had become firmer grassland. Slowly the animal had also changed to meet these new conditions.

It became larger, though still under a metre in height, with three hoofed toes on each foot. Today this animal is known as the mesohippus (middle left).

Much later it evolved into the protohippus (bottom left). As its name suggests, it was the prototype of the horse we see today. It had developed hooves, with the two outer toes on each foot clear of the ground. It was the size of a donkey today.

As far as early man was concerned, the horse was simply another wild animal that could be hunted and killed for food. As man's intelligence improved, he realised that he could tame and train these animals to work.

We know that from very early times the big horses which today are called shires were used to pull carts and work on farms.

In medieval times, when knights, clad in iron and steel, rode out to battle, they were mounted on powerful shire horses, for only they could carry such heavy burdens and gallop at the same time.

Much smaller than the big shires are the ponies. Below right is a Welsh cob which makes an ideal children's pony. It is descended from the native ponies of Wales, a hilly land where in earlier days, ponies were sadly often used in the coal pits. It is small and light enough to climb, yet at the same time strong and sturdy.

The black Arab horse developed in a hotter climate and is lighter than the shire and faster than either a shire or pony. Today it is famous world wide for its success on race courses. Its noble appearance and bearing make it a favourite everywhere. Winners of great races such as the Epsom Derby are worth hundreds of thousands of pounds.

ZEBRAS

Zebras are a type of wild horse. They are black-and-white striped, but no two zebras are striped identically. They live in the eastern, central and southern parts of Africa. They prefer to live on the plains but some groups live in mountain regions.

Their shoulder height is from 1.2 to 1.4 metres. They have upright manes and hairy tails. Zebras roam in herds of varying sizes, some of many hundreds. They will mingle with the herds of other animals such as ostriches or wildebeest. Old zebras, though,

often prefer to live alone. They may live for about twenty-eight years.

They are very inquisitive animals and this weakness often leads them into danger. Lions are the zebras' deadly enemies for the big cats are very fond of eating zebra-meat. Zebras can run at up to 64.5 kilometres per hour. Even without their speed, they would not be easy prey. They protect themselves from attack by biting at their enemies with their front teeth and kicking and slashing with their hind legs. In springtime the mare gives birth to one foal.

There are three types of zebra. Burchell's zebras live in southern and eastern Africa, Grevy's zebras live in the north-east region while the Mountain zebra, with its reddish nose, roams in the mountain areas of southern Africa. Some zebras are protected in wild-life sanctuaries and also in zoos.

WILD PIGS

Thousands of years ago, all pigs were wild, forest animals. Man tamed them and kept them in herds to provide him with food. Now, only a few pigs live wild in the forests.

The ugly warthog of Africa looks more frightening than it really is for, unlike most wild pigs, it prefers to run when attacked. If cornered, though, it can inflict severe wounds with its tusks.

It will, if possible, seek cover by backing into a burrow dug by an aardvark. It gets its name from the warts that are on the sides of the head and in front of the eyes of the male warthog.

Like all pigs, it loves to roll in mud. This keeps it cool and the dried mud protects its body from the stings of flies.

It feeds on grass, roots, berries and the bark of young trees. Although its eyesight seems to be poor, it has very acute senses of smell and hearing. Its flesh is very tasty and is much appreciated by local inhabitants.

The biggest of the pig family is the giant forest hog (above). Its shoulder height is from 76 to 96 centimetres and it is from 1.5 to 1.9 metres in length. The male will often charge without warning. Its main food is shrub and tall, lush grass.

The babirusa (below) belongs to Malaysia. Most wild pigs have tusks growing from the sides of the jaw but the babirusa's tusks grow backwards and upwards and are of little use as weapons. The wild pig is a protected species.

RHINOCEROSES

Rhinoceroses have a shoulder height of between 1 and 2 metres. They have huge bodies and weigh 1 to 3.5 tonnes.

They have very thick, almost hairless hides. They are constantly plagued by swarms of ticks and parasites which is why certain birds, particularly tick-birds, are the rhinos' best friends. The birds alight on the backs of the rhinos and eat the insects. Should an intruder approach, the birds chatter and fly away so warning the big beasts of a possible danger. Rhinos live in Java, Borneo, Sumatra and Africa.

The population of rhinos is decreasing yearly. High prices are paid to poachers for the horns of the animals they kill. Some people believe the horns contain certain medicinal properties.

The black rhinoceros, often seen roaming in pairs, has two horns on its snout. The front horn is the larger and can be 1.3 metres long. The offspring of the rhino remain with their parents until they are half-grown.

Rhinos remain near waterholes for they live in very hot countries. Other rhinos are the white, the great one-horned and the Javan.

HIPPOPOTAMUSES

There are two types of hippopotamuses, one big and one pygmy. They both live in Africa.

The big hippos live near water-holes or, better still, deep rivers. The skin of the big hippos is very thick, about 5 centimetres. They can remain in water or in a hot dry temperature on land for long periods. A big hippo weighs from 3 to 4.5 tonnes. Should danger threaten, it will swiftly head for deep water and there it will stay for hours on end.

They are very good swimmers and divers. They will stay under the water for three to five minutes at a time, sometimes as long as half an hour. Due to their great weight they can also walk about on the bottom of a river.

Big hippos usually remain in the water during daylight and only come out to feed after night has fallen. They will wander around eating vegetation, particularly the grass and reeds that line the river banks. Often they will travel for many kilometres.

Big hippos will fight each other and use their large teeth to inflict wounds.

When a young hippo is born it will weigh from 27 to 45 kilogrammes. It can swim before it can walk and it remains close to its mother under water. The mother is devoted to her calf and takes great care of it. A calf will often clamber on to its mother's back and bask in the sun while she floats on the surface. In this way the calf is safe from the possible attack of a crocodile.

Hippos are frequently killed for their meat by the local inhabitants. The flesh tastes like that of wild pigs. Left to live its life out, though, big hippos live for up to fifty years.

Pygmy hippos which live in western Africa are only a quarter of the size of the big hippos. They do not spend as much time in the water, nor do they live as long.

Above: *Bactrian camel.*

CAMELS

Camels are famous for their ability to eat and drink sufficiently large quantities to survive without further food and water when they travel for weeks across vast deserts.

In Arabia the dromedary, which has one hump, is used to transport goods and riders across the desert. The Bactrian camel, with two humps, lives wild in the Gobi Desert of Mongolia but is also used as a pack animal.

In the past the camels were much more widely spread and of many different types. The two species of camels alive today live in deserts and have evolved to be adapted to these environments. No other animal has feet like the camel. They only have two toes on each foot, but each toe is wide and flat with a soft pad of flesh on its underside. As the camel walks the toes splay out. This spreads the weight of the camel evenly, so that it can walk on soft sand into which other animals would sink.

Both types of camels also have long eyelashes to keep desert dust and sand out of their eyes. They can also close their nostrils to stop their noses becoming clogged during a sandstorm. The upper lips of camels have a tough pad which is used to crop desert grass and leaves from stout bushes.

The humps are fat stores which enable the camels to survive without food for weeks. Water is not stored in the hump but in the stomach lining.

Above: *Dromedaries in Arabia.*

62

Even when they are carrying heavy loads, camels can travel up to 50 kilometres in a single day. They were one of the first hoofed animals to be tamed by humans. Unlike horses, they run by swinging both legs on one side forward at the same time.

ROE DEER

Above: The head of a doe.

Left: The head of a buck

Below: A newly-born fawn

Roe deer are the smallest deer in Europe, only about 90 centimetres at the shoulder.

The bucks (male deer) have short antlers, up to 30 centimetres long. Strangely the antlers drop off at the end of the year and grow back again in February. In this respect they are different from other species of deer who lose their antlers in spring and grow them again in summer.

When a deer's antlers first grow they are soft and tender and covered with a thin, velvety skin. Later, this thin skin is rubbed off but no bleeding takes place and nor does the animal seem to feel any discomfort.

In the summertime the roe deer is bright red in colour, similar to a fox. It has no white tail patch. In winter, though, it changes its colour to a dark greyish hue and its tail is quite white.

Roe deer do not usually gather together in herds but live as families. It is their custom to live in dark woods close to fields or grassland. During the daytime they cleverly hide themselves in undergrowth. They come out at night to feed. Now and then, in wet weather, a country walker will sometimes come across a roe deer's hoofprints. Seldom will that country walker ever see the animal itself.

One or two young, known as kids, are usually born to a doe (female deer). Young bucks do not start to grow their antlers until they are one or two years old. Does do not have antlers.

Below: *A roe deer's hoofprints are called slots.*

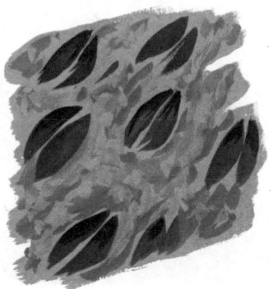

GIRAFFES

The giraffe is without doubt the tallest animal in the world. An adult giraffe can measure 4 metres in height and weigh 550 to 1800 kilogrammes. Like most mammals it has seven neck vertebrae but the giraffe's neck bones are very long.

The giraffe lives in Africa, south of the Sahara Desert. The open scrub and grassland, where there are trees and tasty shrubs it can eat, is where the giraffe makes its home. Here, too, its mottled coat, long limbs and narrow body blend best with the moving patches of shadow and the spindly trunks and branches of the trees. When they stand quite still, giraffes are often mistaken for old, gnarled, forest trees, their bodies being hidden by the bushes and their long legs looking like tree trunks.

The giraffe has very good eyesight and, because of its height, it can see for a long distance. At the first sign of danger, a whole herd of giraffes will gallop away. They can run at a speed of 48 kilometres an hour or more so it is difficult for hungry lions to overtake them. A herd will consist of about fifty giraffes.

They eat leaves and their long necks help them to reach the juicy leaves at the tops of the trees. They have very long tongues, up to 45 centimetres long, with which they can grasp and tear off leaves. A giraffe can do without water for many weeks as long as it has enough juicy leaves to eat.

When it does go for a drink, it is faced with some difficulty. Even its long neck does not help it to reach the water easily. It has to place its forelegs far apart, then bend them at the knees, before it can drink.

A giraffe does not like to get wet. It will neither swim nor wade through a river in its path and it shelters under the trees when it rains.

Apart from man, the lion is the giraffe's only enemy. However, even a lion will rarely attack a lone giraffe because a giraffe is able to defend itself fiercely.

One blow from the powerful hoof of a giraffe can kill a lion and the only giraffe a lion can kill on its own is a young one which has strayed from the herd.

When two giraffes fight, they use their heads as clubs, banging their long necks against each other, until at last the victorious giraffe has completely dazed its opponent.

Usually, giraffes sleep standing up. Only occasionally do they sleep lying down and this is because it is difficult for them to get up again. They rest during the day and search for food in the evenings and early mornings. They feed almost entirely on leaves from the acacia, mimosa and wild apricot trees.

A female giraffe gives birth to one offspring that is able to stand within half an hour of birth.

PANDAS

Giant pandas (below) live in the Chinese provinces of Szechwan, Sikang, Shenshan and Kansu. They measure 1.2 to l.5 metres in length and weigh 75 to 160 kilogrammes. Their coats are thick and woolly, and black and white in colour. Their eye patches, ears, legs and shoulders are black. The rest of the body is off-white. It is thought by some people to be a type of bear, by others to be a member of the raccoon family.

Pandas are solitary creatures and very rare. Just over a hundred years ago they were unknown in Europe, although a few of their pelts were brought to Europe in the eighteenth and nineteenth centuries.

The giant panda's placid nature and its amusing behaviour as a cub make it one of the most popular animals in any zoo. Even so, it becomes very fierce when aroused.

Unlike bears, giant pandas do not hibernate and are alert and active throughout the year. If pursued by dogs, they will rapidly climb trees but usually they live on the ground. They make their homes in caves, hollow trees or rock crevices.

They feed from ten to twelve hours each

day. Their favourite food is bamboo shoots up to 13 millimetres thick as well as the roots of the bamboo. They eat other plants such as crocuses, irises and grass tufts. They are not vegetarians, though, as they will eat fish and small rodents.

One or two cubs are usually born to a giant panda in January. Each weighs about 2 kilogrammes when born. In captivity they are fed on bamboo shoots, vegetables, milk, rolled oats and cod liver oil.

Another type of panda, not so well-known but more numerous, is the lesser, or red panda which is about half the size of a giant panda.

Unlike the giant panda, the red panda has a long tail and looks quite friendly. It is, in fact, a very fierce creature and can inflict a terrible bite. Red pandas have razor-sharp claws and can move swiftly. They are good climbers and make their homes in holes in trees. They spend much of their time foraging on the ground for food.

They live in the areas which stretch from the west of Nepal to Yunnan and Szechwan in China, as shown in the map at the top of the page.

The detailed face of a red panda

TAPIRS

Tapirs look somewhat like very small elephants with, instead of long trunks, short snouts. They like eating branches and twigs that they pull from trees. They live in woodland, close to some form of water supply. They hide in the woods during the daytime but leave their shelter to feed on grassy areas away from the trees.

There are four different types of tapirs: firstly, the Asiatic type which lives in Burma, Thailand, the Malay States and Sumatra; secondly, there are the Brazilian tapirs of Colombia, Venezuela and Brazil; thirdly, the Andean tapirs that range in the mountains of Colombia and Ecuador; lastly, there are the tapirs known as Baird's tapirs which inhabit southern Mexico southwards to Colombia and Ecuador.

Tapirs are about the size of a donkey. Their shoulder height is about a metre, and they can weigh as much as 300 kilogrammes.

The front half of the Asiatic tapir (above) is blackish as are its hind legs. It looks quite different from the other three types which have bodies that are reddish or dark brown above and paler below. Young tapirs are dark with bright white and yellow stripes and spots. After six to eight months the stripes and spots disappear.

Tapirs sleep close to the banks of rivers and lakes. They frequently live alone or in pairs and are very agile indeed. They are good swimmers and divers, hill-climbers and runners. They love to wallow in mud or relax in water.

They are not vicious animals and if threatened will make for a nearby river and dive into the water to hide, or race for the shelter of woodland. If trapped, though, they defend themselves by biting.

The animals which kill and eat the tapirs of South America are jaguars. In Asia, tigers are their greedy killers. In mountain areas, tapirs have to beware of bears.

Chapter Two
BIRDS

All birds have feathers and wings and lay eggs. Most birds can fly. A few cannot. Birds' feathers grow from their skin just as hair grows on mammals. The feathers, though, grow to a certain length, become old and fall out. Then new ones replace them. This cycle is called moulting. It happens once a year.

Most birds mate in the spring. They build nests in which the females lay their eggs. Parent birds take care of the eggs, ensuring that the eggs are never exposed to hot sun or to the cool air of night until, in due course, the eggs hatch.

KINGFISHERS

Kingfishers live all over the world. There are many different kinds. The British common kingfishers (above) are the most brilliantly coloured of all European birds. They nest in burrows which they dig in the banks of rivers. They will sit on branches overhanging rivers and wait for a fish. When the fish passes by, the kingfisher streaks down into the river, catches the fish in its beak and flies to a branch of a tree to eat the fish.

Other types of kingfishers are insect-eaters.

SWANS

Here is the graceful swan. It is called a mute swan because its only sound is a soft hiss. Wild swans are fierce but tame swans are usually quite friendly.

At nesting time, the male swan, called a cob, becomes very protective. It will keep away any other water-fowl from its nesting area. A blow from the wing of a swan can break a person's leg.

Swans' nests are large, untidy and made with reeds, sticks and leaves. The female, called a pen, lays between five and eight pale-green eggs. The young swans are called cygnets. At first they have greyish-brown feathers and look like balls of brown fluff. These feathers lighten in colour as the year progresses and the following spring the plumage is that of an adult swan.

The swan's long neck, which is as long as its body, helps it to reach food on a shallow river bed. It eats water-plants and insects. Swans' wings measure 4.5 metres.

WOODPECKERS

Should you be walking in a forest or wood one day, you may hear a strange tapping noise if you listen. More than likely you are listening to a woodpecker's beak as the bird taps it on the bark of a tree to bore a hole. The woodpecker is in search of insects, or maybe it is drilling a hole in the trunk in which to build its nest and lay its eggs.

By boring holes, the woodpecker is able to get at the soft, white grubs of wood-boring beetles. These beetles would certainly cause great damage to the tree.

When a pair of woodpeckers wants a home, they can make a deep hole in a tree-trunk as quickly as a man can do it with a hammer and chisel.

On the chips of wood that fall to the bottom of the hole, the female lays her glossy, white eggs. When the chicks hatch they are blind and naked but after two weeks their eyes are open and they have grown feathers. When they are old enough to fly they soon learn to search for insects which they scoop up on their long, sticky tongues.

The bird shown here is a greater spotted woodpecker. There is also a lesser spotted and a green woodpecker.

BARN OWLS

There are about one hundred and thirty types of owls living around the world. All owls have large eyes and feed on small animals. Most owls hunt at night, but a few are active in daylight.

The barn owl is found on nearly all land-masses, except parts of Asia. It is a highly skilled hunter which preys on small rodents, birds and some of the larger insects. It has superb eyesight, enabling it to hunt on the darkest nights. However, the barn owl does not rely on sight alone. It has very sharp hearing which allows it to locate a mouse by the sound it makes moving through long

Above: *An adult barn owl with its distinctive, tawny back and snow-white underside.*
Right: *Barn owl chicks are helpless and rely on their parents for food.*
Facing page: *A barn owl glides silently over the fields in search of prey.*

74

grass. The flight of this owl, like that of most others, is almost silent. The edges of the feathers are fluffy, breaking up the airflow which creates the swishing sound made by the wings of other birds.

Like all owls, the barn owl swallows its prey whole, later coughing up a pellet composed of the unwanted skin and bones of its victims.

Barn owls build nests in hollow trees and empty buildings. The nest is made from the fur and bones of their prey. About five eggs are laid in the early spring. They hatch after five weeks and the young are fed by both parents until the autumn when they leave the nest and hunt for their own food. In recent years the numbers of barn owls have been declining in Europe, but not elsewhere.

SPARROWS

Sparrows must be the most well-known of all birds. There are two kinds; the house sparrow and the tree sparrow.

The house sparrow is the more common of the two. As its name indicates it can be seen all the time in gardens close to houses and farms.

The male house sparrow has a black bib and dark grey crown. The hen is brown. House sparrows make their nests in many places, often in walls or barns, under eaves or in creepers, as well as in bushes and trees. They lay their eggs, five or six at a time, during the six months from February to August.

Both kinds of sparrow feed on seeds, grain and insects.

Tree sparrows (above) are slightly smaller than house sparrows. They have a smaller black bib and a brown cap. Cocks and hens look alike.

In its habits, it is quite different from the house sparrow. It prefers the open country-side to the town and stays well clear of human dwellings.

Tree sparrows tend to live in colonies. They make their nests in holes in old walls, in hedgerows and in trees. Here they lay four to six eggs from April to June.

GOLDFINCHES

There are several types of finches; hawfinches, greenfinches, bullfinches and chaffinches. Goldfinches are the most beautiful. They like weedy places and are welcomed by farmers for they eat thistles, groundsel and other harmful weed seeds.

They may choose an orchard to build their nests and lay four to six eggs in May.

BOWERBIRDS

There are eighteen species of bowerbirds, all of which live in New Guinea or Australia. They take their name from their habit of building elaborate bowers on the forest floor. The bower is built by the male and is used to attract a female. The eggs are laid, and the chicks raised, in a small nest some distance from the bower. Each species builds a different type of bower. The great grey bowerbird builds a simple corridor of woven grass, but the striped gardener bowerbird erects a tent-like canopy of twigs and grass which may be over a metre across.

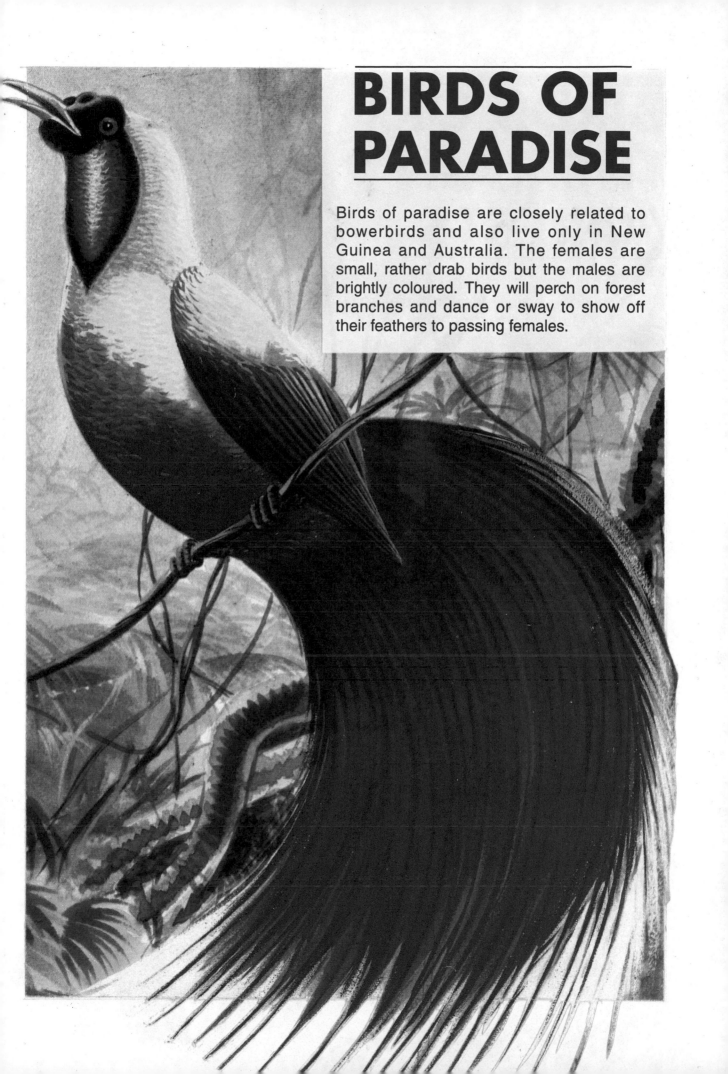

BIRDS OF PARADISE

Birds of paradise are closely related to bowerbirds and also live only in New Guinea and Australia. The females are small, rather drab birds but the males are brightly coloured. They will perch on forest branches and dance or sway to show off their feathers to passing females.

BIRDS OF THE RAIN FORESTS

More rain falls in a single day on the forests of India, Malaysia, Africa and South America than falls in Europe in a full year. In these forests the trees grow very tall. Their leaves keep out the sun and few plants grow on the ground. The flowers and fruits grow higher up and this is where the many birds are found.

The floors of these forests are thick with rotting leaves and branches and teem with armies of ants marching. Ahead of the ants, an ant bird (above) is waiting to feed on the insects. Some ant birds stay with an army of ants for several days.

Manakins (below left) often join the ant

birds. The cock birds have special feathers which make loud cracking noises when they want to attract a mate.

Orioles live in the forests of Africa and South America. They fly in the tree tops hunting for caterpillars. Their nests are slung like hammocks between two branches. (Page 80 bottom right)

Touracos (above) live mainly in the rain forests while others live in the bushlands of South Africa. Strangely, the touracos' red feathers will dye water red, but rain does not cause the birds' feathers to drip red water. Another strange thing about this bird is that it can run along branches like a squirrel.

Toucans (below left) are found only in the forests of South America. The bills, or beaks, are very light. With them toucans tear fruit from plants and then toss it down their throats. Toucans sometimes play at fencing with their bills and throw fruit at each other. When a toucan goes to sleep it buries its bill along its back and lifts its tail forwards.

The harpy eagle (below right) has the strongest talons of any of the birds of prey. It is greatly feared by the smaller birds of the rain forests.

OSTRICHES

Ostriches are the largest, living birds, averaging about 2.7 metres in height. They live on the open plains of Africa where they feed on seeds and fruits together with lizards and insects. Ostriches cannot fly, but they can run extremely quickly. It is thought that they can reach 70 kilometres per hour over short distances. The ostriches rely on this speed to escape hunters such as lions and leopards. Ostriches have been farmed for some years. The long feathers are used in the fashion trade while the meat is becoming increasingly popular. Some farmers in Europe and North America have begun raising ostriches.

FACT FILE - OSTRICHES

The egg of an ostrich is the largest in the world, it could contain 40 hen's eggs.
Ostriches can be trained to act as 'sheepdogs', 'scarecrows' and even as 'racehorses'.

EMUS

Emus are large, flightless birds which live in Australia. They can stand up to 2 metres in height, and are extremely muscular. The birds are adapted to the vast, open plains of central Australia where they find the seeds, fruits and insects on which they feed. The female builds a nest by scraping a hole in the ground in which she lays her eight or nine eggs, but it is the male which sits on them for over seven weeks. In recent years emus have been considered a pest by farmers because they trample down crops and eat large quantities of grain. Despite being extensively hunted, emus remain fairly numerous.

PENGUINS

Penguins are birds that cannot fly. There are eighteen different species. They are all splendid swimmers and can propel themselves through the water at a rate of 30 kilometres per hour. They live only in the southern seas of the world, on the islands off Australia, in New Zealand, South Africa and southern South America. Those that live in the snow and ice cannot build nests.

The biggest are the Emperor penguins (left) which stand about 1.2 metres and weigh about 75 kilogrammes. When a female lays an egg, it is the male that keeps it off the ice by resting it on top of his feet. When the chick hatches, the male, which will not have eaten for two months, then goes off to feed while the female stays with the chick to feed and protect it.

Adelie penguins (below) gather in huge colonies, sometimes as many as half a million in one group.

Rockhopper penguins (left) are so called because of the way they hop from rock to rock. They have long crests on their heads. Their chicks are covered with soft down when hatched. They are helpless at first and need to be looked after and fed for several weeks.

As far back as 1499 it was noted that the jackass penguin (right) brayed like an ass. It is also known as the black-footed penguin.

Gentoo penguins (above) live on many of the Antarctic islands. They are very friendly and do not fear man.

King penguins (below) also live in the Antarctic. They toboggan on their stomachs at great speed on the ice to escape their enemies.

HUMMING-BIRDS

Humming-birds live in South and Central America.

Bee humming-birds are the smallest birds in the world and are not much larger than a bumble-bee. They build tiny nests out of spiders' webs and moss in which to lay eggs just 8 millimetres long.

BIRDS' NESTS

WEAVER-BIRDS

Weaver-birds take their name from the way they weave their nests.

The nest of the baya weaver-bird is built out of grass and leaves by the male to attract a female.

The small entrance is through the tube at the bottom. The nest protects the eggs from rats and other predators.

FACT FILE - BIRDS' NESTS

The Chinese make a soup from the nest of a particular variety of swift.

The common guillemot has no nest. It lays its egg on a rock ledge on a cliff.

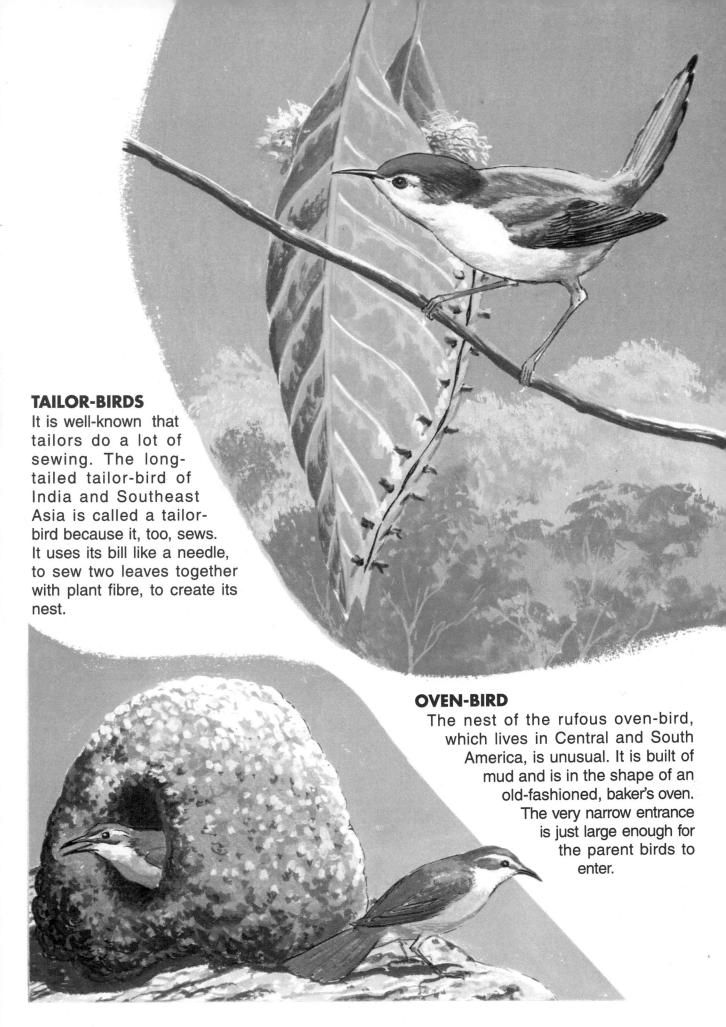

TAILOR-BIRDS

It is well-known that tailors do a lot of sewing. The long-tailed tailor-bird of India and Southeast Asia is called a tailor-bird because it, too, sews. It uses its bill like a needle, to sew two leaves together with plant fibre, to create its nest.

OVEN-BIRD

The nest of the rufous oven-bird, which lives in Central and South America, is unusual. It is built of mud and is in the shape of an old-fashioned, baker's oven. The very narrow entrance is just large enough for the parent birds to enter.

ROBINS

The robin is probably the best-known of all British birds, especially at Christmas time when it can be seen on so many greeting cards. Its red breast stands out strikingly against a white, snowy background.

It has a cheerful song, a handsome appearance and is so friendly that it will often hop on to a windowsill inside a house, to feed on nuts or even a piece of cheese, when it gets to know you.

The robin measures about 140 millimetres from beak to tail and has a wingspan of about 180 millimetres.

Robins choose many different places for their nests. As well as bushes they will choose holes in walls or trees. They have been known to choose an old rusty pan, a letterbox, a boot, an old car and even a pulpit.

Their nests are bulky and made of moss and grass and lined with hair and feathers. Both the cock and the hen help to make the nest and take turns sitting on the eggs to hatch them. They both rear their young.

Five or six eggs are laid around March and these are white, speckled with pale red. They take about two weeks to hatch.

Robins chiefly feed on insects, including spiders and fleas, but they also eat worms, berries and seeds.

Chapter Three
FISH

There are freshwater and sea-water fish. How do they live when they spend their time in the water? They breathe oxygen which is in the water.

A fish takes in water every time it opens its mouth. Its body absorbs the oxygen in the water into the blood system. It then filters the used water out through its gills which are usually at the back of its head on either side of its body.

Fish use their fins to propel them through the water, as stabilisers and as rudders.

CLIMBING PERCH

Perch are freshwater fish. They move in shoals and are greedy eaters. They eat worms, small fish and other smaller perch. They gather from March until May to spawn and lay their eggs along river-beds. The climbing perch is the most interesting perch. It is found in Asia and crawls over mud-flats in search of food.

RIVER FISH

Many different types of fish live in the fresh water of rivers and lakes. Freshwater fish feed on all sorts of food. Some eat water plants, while others feed on water insects and shellfish. A few species prey on other fish and are formidable hunters.

Some species of freshwater fish are found in only one lake or one river because they are unable to move to other areas. However, a few fish are found in many different places. Sometimes fish eggs are carried to a new home by becoming trapped on the feet of waterbirds, or the fish may be moved by humans. However, some fish swim to other rivers. The salmon (above), when it is about four years old, leaves its river for the open sea. After two or more years at sea it returns to lay eggs. Most salmon return to their own rivers, but a few travel to other rivers.

FACT FILE - RIVER FISH

Caviar is the eggs of the sturgeon. A female may produce seven million eggs.
In Kentucky a system of caves has its own species of fish which is completely blind.

The chub lives in the lakes and rivers of Europe. It feeds on water plants and small invertebrates (any animals that have no backbone) whilst swimming slowly through quiet water. Chub grow to about 4 kilogrammes in weight.

Perch are found in Europe and northern Asia. They hide among water weeds, but will dart out to snatch a passing fish. There are about a hundred and twenty types of perch.

The pike is a powerful hunter in rivers of Europe, North America and Asia. It grows to a length of about 1.5 metres and preys on small water-birds as well as on most types of river fish.

91

SEA FISH

Of all the fish in the sea, the swordfish (above) is probably the most powerful for its size, and it is one of the fastest swimmers. Fully grown it is between 5 and 6 metres in length and weighs a tonne. Swordfish have often pierced ships' hulls.

Why swordfish attack whales is a mystery. It is thought that a sword-fish streaking towards a whale may be unable to stop before piercing its body. Another idea is that a swordfish, sighting a whale and fearful of the whale's size, will attack first.

A very different fish is the seahorse (below). Its eyes move independently of each other. It often remains quite still with its tail wrapped around the stem of a plant.

The sting-ray (above) is an unwelcome catch for a fisherman. It has a long and whip-like tail which it uses to defend itself. Along its tail there is a projecting spine which can inflict a dangerous wound on a human. When a fisherman by chance catches a sting-ray he will first cut off its tail. He will then remove the sting-ray's liver because from it an oil can be extracted which is suitable for use in lamps. The rest of the fish is thrown away.

It is easy to recognise an angler fish (below) because it is not only at least 2 metres long but it has a huge, gaping mouth.

The angler fish does not have to search for food. It has several filaments projecting from its back. At the end of the first filament is a flap of shiny skin which the angler fish waves thus luring an unsuspecting fish to swim towards its large mouth and those waiting teeth.

AQUARIUM FISH

Many people keep fish in aquariums as a hobby. An aquarium is a glass-sided tank of water.

The water is kept warm by a heater and aerated by a pump which blows air bubbles into the water. Without warmth and oxygen in the water the fish would die. Fish with bright colours or odd habits are most popular. Some are wild species, but some are specially bred from captive fish.

Above: *A flame fish (left) and a tiger barb (right).*

Above: *The brightly marked paradise fish which has been carefully bred in captivity to produce the red stripes and deep blue colouring which make it so popular.*

Above: *Two popular aquarium fish. On the left is the three-spot damselfish and on the right is the cardinal tetra, named because it is the same colour as a cardinal's cloak.*

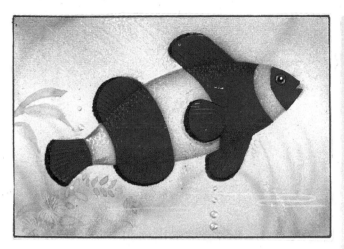

Above: *The clown fish which lives wild among the coral reefs of the Pacific Ocean.*

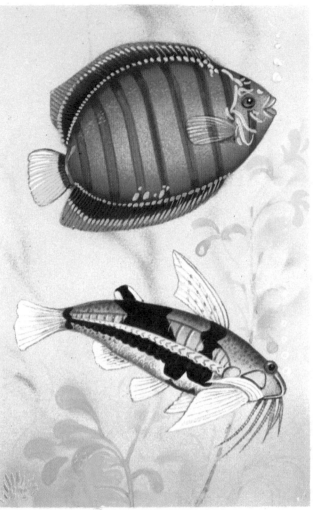

Above: *At the top of the picture is a pompadour fish, named after a famous French lady who lived two hundred and fifty years ago, and below it a talking catfish.*

Above: *An angel fish, perhaps the most popular aquarium fish because it is easy to keep.*

Above: *A lionfish which should only be kept by experienced people as it is poisonous.*

Above: *A goldfish. Goldfish were first bred in China in the seventh century.*

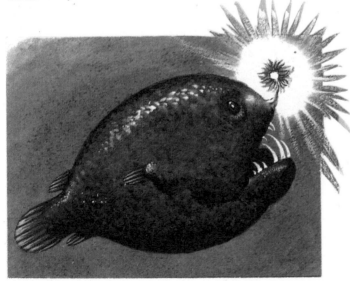

Trunkfish

Grunt Sculpin

Deep-sea Angler Fish

ODD FISH

Fish have lived on Earth for over four hundred million years. During that time they have evolved into many different types, of various shapes and sizes. Some fish have scales; some do not. Some have gills; some do not. Generally speaking, however, a fish is a cold-blooded creature with a backbone, gills and a heart.

Today there are about forty-four thousand different types of fish, probably more. Among these many types of fish there are a few which are quite unlike any other. Some of these odd fish are shown here.

The trunkfish is encased in bony armour that protects it from hunters.

The grunt sculpin (middle) lives on the bottom of shallow waters off the coasts of the North Atlantic. Instead of swimming, it uses its fins to 'walk' along the mud.

The deep-sea angler fish (bottom) lives in the eternal darkness of waters far beneath the surface. It uses the luminous growth to lure small fish within range of its jaws.

Damselfish

Chinesefish

Upsidedown Catfish

The Chinesefish (above) habitually swims upright, its tail pointing downwards and its mouth near the surface to snap up food.

The damselfish (top right) is immune to the stings of the sea anemone and can hide from predators in the deadly tentacles.

The catfish (middle) swims either way up and is called an "upsidedown catfish".

The flying fish (bottom) lives in tropical oceans around the world. It uses its long fins to act as wings to allow it to glide up to 40 metres through the air. It probably takes to the air to escape predators.

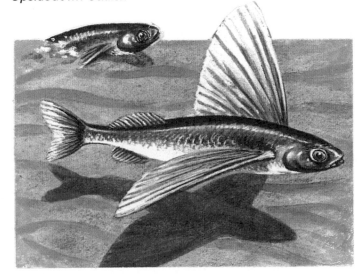

Flying fish

97

SHARKS

Sharks are flesh-eating fish so one can easily understand why they are the most feared by all human swimmers.

The giant white sharks are very fast and ferocious and attack anything that moves. The blue sharks and tiger sharks are also deadly killers.

Different from them are the whale sharks which are the largest of all fish.

They eat small animals and plants. The porbeagle shark (above) eats mackerel, haddock, cod and dogfish. These fish are all swallowed whole.

The porbeagle is about 3 metres in length. It is a great nuisance so far as fishermen are concerned for sometimes porbeagles are caught in nets that are already partly filled with other fish. A porbeagle so caught will promptly break through the net so releasing the rest of the catch. The porbeagle is easily recognised by its pointed snout.

Chapter Four
INSECTS

Of all the creatures living on earth, about eighty per cent are insects. Over one million are known to zoologists. Thousands more are discovered every year. To give some idea of their rate of production, a female cabbage aphid has about forty offspring. Each one of these is mature enough to have offspring in two weeks. Some termites lay one egg every two seconds for twenty-four hours a day.

There are large and small insects. Stick insects are more than 30 centimetres in length. Some beetles are smaller than pin-heads. Others are 15 centimetres long.

LOCUSTS

Locusts are a species of grasshoppers. They will gather in huge swarms which are greatly feared by all farmers for they destroy any plants that lie in their path. Some swarms have been known to average a kilometre in height, 160 kilometres in width and 450 kilometres in length.

By rubbing their wings together, locusts make a distinctive noise so you can imagine the thunder that millions of these insects make when flying.

BEETLES

The beetle is an insect and the beetle family consists of over three thousand different types of beetles.

The stag beetle (left) is the largest beetle found in Great Britain and Europe. It grows to a length of about 10 centimetres. The stag beetle is so called because the male's jaws look rather like the horns of a stag. It has wings and can fly. Although the male's jaws look quite powerful the smaller jaws of the female (bottom left) are much stronger. As a real stag fights with its horns, so does a stag beetle when it is defending its own territory. The larvae of the stag beetle feed on rotting wood in the roots of dead or dying trees.

In the bottom right-hand picture a larva is curled up in a rotting tree trunk. It stays in the tree for as long as four years. It then changes into a pupa, which is the last stage of development, before emerging as a young beetle.

Ladybirds, like many other insects, fly. They are found all over Europe and America. They consume vast numbers of other insects and pests that eat the crops on which we live. Like the stag beetle, the life-cycle is from egg to larva to pupa to beetle.

Ladybirds vary in colour, size and their pattern of spots, as can be seen from the different varieties shown here.

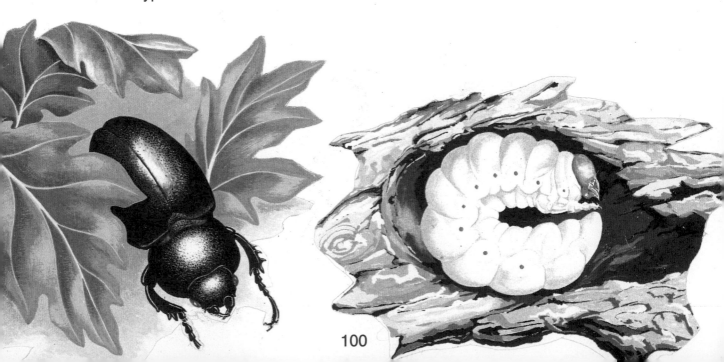

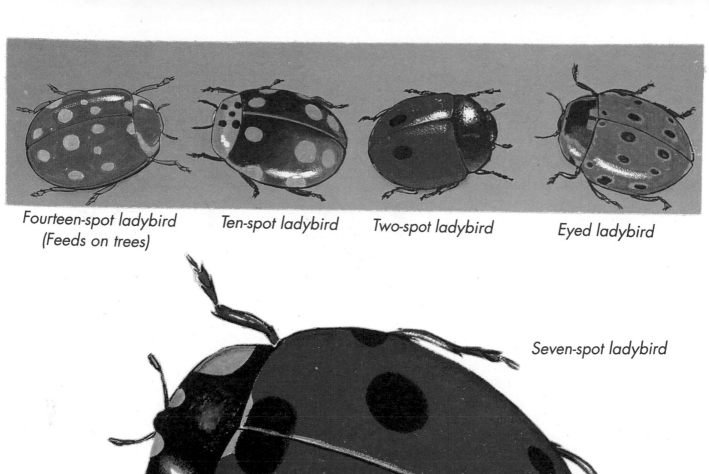

Fourteen-spot ladybird
(Feeds on trees)

Ten-spot ladybird

Two-spot ladybird

Eyed ladybird

Seven-spot ladybird

Larva

Twice-stabbed ladybird

Nine-spot ladybird

Fourteen-spot ladybird
(Feeds on plants)

Ten-spot ladybird

BEES

Bees are insects that belong to the Hymenoptera order, which also includes ants and wasps. Most bees live together in groups of several thousand. Each bee co-operates with its fellows for the mutual benefit of the group, or hive.

An artificial beehive (left) is where domestic bees are cared for by bee-keepers. These bees are kept so that the humans can take the honey which the bees make and store as food for the winter. The honey is made by worker bees, which make up the majority of the hive. Workers (above) are immature, female bees. There is one mature female in each hive, called the queen, who lays eggs. Workers (below left) visit flowers near the hive to gather pollen and nectar. The material is taken back to the hive (below). If a worker has found a particularly good group of flowers, it will perform a dance which tells the other workers how to find the flowers. The pollen and nectar are then processed into honey.

In the hive, the bees build a lattice-work of hexagonal cells called a comb. The walls of the comb are made of wax. Combs are used to store honey to provide food for the bees in winter.

Some combs are used to rear young bees. The queen lays an egg in each cell. After the egg hatches, the young bee stays in the cell for several weeks. During this time it is fed by the worker bees.

The bumble-bee (below) builds its nest underground, in a burrow built by a mouse or bird. In the autumn all the bees die except the queen which survives to found a new nest the following spring.

The head of a bumble-bee, (right) showing the long tongue used to gather nectar.

WASPS

There are several thousand different types of wasps. Their colours range from dull black or brown to brilliant red and yellow and blue. The colours warn birds not to eat these dangerous insects.

Wasps feed on a variety of foods. Some feed on fruit and other plant foods. Most of these wasps live in nests in which several thousand wasps may be found. Wasp nests are built by the queen wasp in early spring. She constructs the nest out of paper made by chewing dead wood. The queen wasp lays several eggs, which hatch into worker wasps which go out to collect food. All through the summer the worker wasps are hatched and search for food but during the autumn the queen stops laying eggs. The workers die and the queen abandons the nest to find a place where she can sleep through the winter.

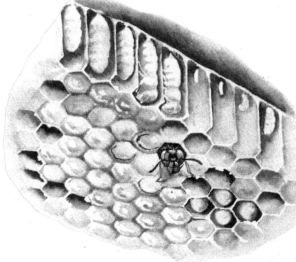

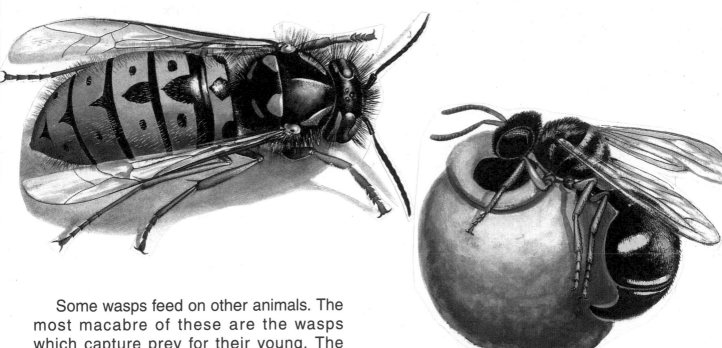

Some wasps feed on other animals. The most macabre of these are the wasps which capture prey for their young. The Pepsis wasp is a species of spider wasp. It preys on spiders, often attacking them in their own homes. When the female Pepsis wasp is ready to breed it digs a hole and paralyses a spider by stinging it. The spider is then pushed into the hole and an egg laid on it. When the egg hatches it has its own ready source of meat on which to feed. Potter wasps use a similar technique. They build a nest out of mud in which they lay a single egg. The wasp then hunts for a number of caterpillars which are placed in the pot. The pot is sealed and the wasp larva feeds on the paralysed caterpillars.

Facing page top: *A cross section of an underground wasp nest to show the entrance tunnel and paper construction;* **(bottom left)** *wasps eating juicy plums and* **(bottom right)** *worker wasp larvae in their paper cells.*
Above left: *A worker wasp from a communal species.*
Above: *A potter wasp constructs its nest.*
Below left: *A sand wasp smooths the top of its nest with a small pebble.*
Below: *The Pepsis, a type of spider wasp.*

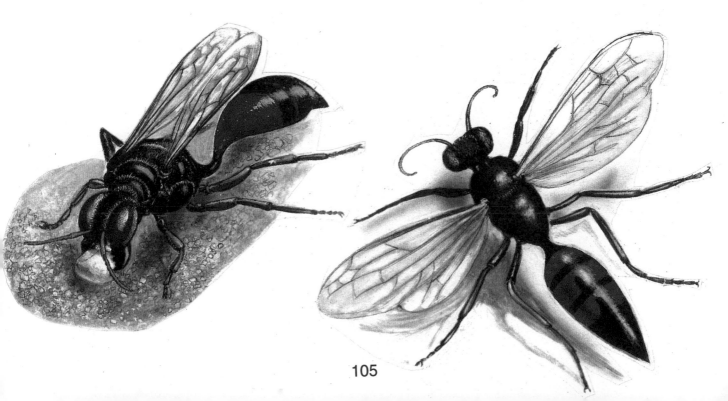

ANTS

One of the most successful groups of insects are the ants. There are over ten thousand different types of ants which live all over the world. Scientists place all ants in the family Formicidae and it is thought that they are related to bees and wasps more closely than to other insects.

Ants all live in large nests in which several thousand will live and work together to provide food, safety and warmth. The centre of all ants' nests is the queen, or a fully-grown female. The queen does no actual work, but is fed and cared for by the workers. She spends her entire life laying eggs, which will hatch out into more workers.

Within the nest, different workers have different jobs to perform. Some workers

guard the entrance to the nest. These workers often have large jaws with which to attack any insects which try to enter the nest. Other workers stay in the nest all their lives, caring for the eggs and larvae produced by the queen. But most workers gather food from the surrounding area. Most ants eat a variety of foods, including leaves and other insects, but a few species concentrate on just a single type of food.

Several species of ant have the curious habit of farming aphids. Aphids are tiny insects which feed on the sap of green plants. As they feed, the aphids excrete a sweet, sticky substance called honeydew. Ants love this honeydew and lick it off the aphids. Some ants go even further and care for the aphids. The ants will carry young aphids to fresh plants on which to feed and may build shelters to protect the aphids from attack. Ants will stimulate the aphids to produce more honeydew by gently stroking them.

At certain times of the year the queen will lay special eggs. These hatch into adult, winged males and females. Large numbers of these flying ants take off from the nest. They mate on the wing, after which the males quickly die. The females, meanwhile, search for suitable sites for new nests. After gathering some food, they lay eggs which hatch out into workers. These workers form the cores of the new nests while each female becomes the queen of a new nest.

DRAGONFLIES AND DAMSELFLIES

Dragonflies and damselflies are closely related insects which fly strongly on their two pairs of wings. Often the wings are brightly coloured and the insects can be very attractive.

Dragonflies and damselflies are predators. They catch their prey in mid-air by seizing them in their powerful jaws. Their eyes are large and can spot their prey at a great distance.

Eggs are laid in ponds and streams. When an egg hatches it produces a larva, called a nymph, which lives under water for several months. The nymphs are aggressive hunters which attack water insects, worms and even small fish and tadpoles as they grow larger. As it grows, a nymph changes its skin about a dozen times and gradually eats bigger prey. It is able to move very quickly by squirting water backwards in a form of jet propulsion. Eventually, the nymph climbs up a reed or other water plant to emerge into the air. There it breaks out of its skin as a fully-formed, adult dragonfly.

FACT FILE - DRAGONFLIES AND DAMSELFLIES

The fastest insect of all is the Australian dragonfly which can fly at nearly 60 kilometres per hour.
The smallest dragonfly is the Agriocnemis naia found in Burma. It is 1.8 centimetres long.

BUTTERFLIES

Butterflies are insects which belong to the order Lepidoptera, which also includes moths. They have large wings, which are often beautifully coloured, and long, slender bodies. There are thousands of different types of butterfly living all around the world. They vary in size from the Queen Alexandra's birdwing with a wing span of 28 centimetres to the tiny dwarf blue of South Africa that has a wing span of 14 millimetres.

Birdwing Butterfly

South American Morpho Butterfly

South African Red Butterfly

Helen Morpho Butterfly

Peruvian Agrias Butterfly

MOTHS

Moths and butterflies are very much alike in appearance. There are many of each that have beautifully-coloured wings. Moths have thicker bodies than the slender butterflies. There is another major difference. Butterflies like fluttering around in warm sunshine. So, too, do several kinds of moths but most of them fly at night.

It is reckoned that although there are about sixty species of butterflies in Britain and over two thousand species of moths, throughout the world there are more than a hundred thousand species of moths.

The life cycle of moths and butterflies is very similar. Both lay eggs, (from one hundred to three thousand) from which emerge caterpillars. The caterpillars become pupae before changing into delicate-winged insects.

Moths lay their eggs on the leaves of plants. After a month the eggs hatch into caterpillars. The caterpillar's first meal is the eggshell from which it has emerged. It then feeds on the leaf and the rest of the plant. It remains a caterpillar for about two months, and is a pupa for the same length of time.

Above is a crimson speckled moth. It is rarely seen in Britain for it prefers a warmer climate.

On the right is the yellow underwing moth which can be seen from June to September.

Although most moths are quite small the wing-span of the black witch of America is up to 30 centimetres.

Chapter Five
REPTILES

Crocodiles are one of the four different groups of reptiles.

The first group consists of only one animal, the tuatara. It is a protected animal. The second group is made up of turtles and tortoises, the third group by lizards and snakes and the last group by crocodilians.

All reptiles are cold-blooded creatures. Their blood takes on the temperature of the immediate area in which they live. They live happily only in lands where the weather is very hot. Reptiles living in cool climates hibernate in winter.

CROCODILES

The group of crocodilians is made up of crocodiles, alligators, caimans and gavials. They can see easily underwater because they have semi-transparent, third eyelids. They lay eggs which hatch into young crocodiles. There are several kinds of crocodiles, the smallest being the dwarf crocodile which measures only about a metre. The biggest is the Nile crocodile (above). It is reported to be about 8 metres in length.

LIZARDS

Basilisks (above) live in the dense forests of South America. They feed on fruit and insects and grow to be about 75 centimetres long. Basilisks can rear up on their hind legs when they want to run at speed.

FACT FILE - LIZARDS

Lizards are small reptiles with long tails and can generally move very quickly when they need to. Scientifically, the lizards belong to the Squamata order (which also includes snakes), and are divided into twenty families.

The fin-tailed lizard of Java and nearby islands (above) lives in the forests which blanket those hot, humid islands. It finds its food of fruit and insects in the upper branches of these trees. It may grow to reach over a metre in length, but much of this is made up of its tail.

The sand agama (above) can put on a frightening display when it is threatened. It opens its mouth wide and spreads flaps of skin, decorated with tooth-like spikes. Combined with the red colour of the head this makes the creature look much larger and fiercer than it really is and scares off many attackers. There are about two hundred species of agama which live throughout Asia, Africa and Australia, and in parts of Europe.

The sea iguana (left) lives only on the remote Galapagos Islands in the eastern Pacific Ocean. It can grow up to 1.5 metres in length. The sea iguana uses its powerful tail to push it through the water and is the only lizard to live mostly in the sea. It feeds almost exclusively on seaweed, which it must dive to reach off the rocky coast. Male sea iguanas each have a small patch of rocky coast which they defend against other males by head-butting any intruders out of the way.

113

SNAKES

Snakes are reptiles which lack legs. They are closely related to lizards and are thought to have evolved from an early type of lizard about eighty million years ago. Snakes are distinguished from all other reptiles by the ability to dislocate their lower jaws so that they can swallow objects larger than themselves.

The horned rattlesnake shown above is sometimes called a sidewinder because of its method of movement. It pushes itself sideways by throwing out a loop of its body and pulling it in again.

The anaconda on the left lives in the dense forests of South America, usually near to rivers or swamps. It kills its prey by squeezing them until they suffocate. Anacondas often reach 9 metres and may grow much larger.

The dull-green water snake of northern South America spends most of its life in swamps and rivers where it preys on frogs and fish.

The python (above) lives in India and hunts at night, using heat-seeking sensors in its nose to find prey. Its jaws stretch to allow it to swallow whole a wild pig or deer, which forms a large lump in the snake's stomach until it is digested.

Shown on the left are a pair of Indian cobras. These extremely poisonous snakes grow to over 2 metres in length and feed on rats, birds and other small animals. If a cobra feels threatened it will rear up and spread its hood to warn any intruder. If the intruder does not move away, the snake will bite, injecting poison deadly enough to kill an adult human.

TORTOISES AND TERRAPINS

The snapping turtle (above) lives in North and Central America. It takes its name from its habit of lunging with snapping jaws at any passing animals which are small enough to be prey. In early summer it drags itself on to a beach to lay about forty eggs in a hollow in the sand. When the eggs hatch (right) the young turtles are on their own and are not cared for by the mother.

The European pond turtle (right) hunts fish and frogs in ponds and streams. In the winter it hibernates in burrows. The leatherback turtle (below) lays its eggs on sandy beaches. For some unknown reason it will turn around twice after laying its eggs and before it swims away.

The gopher tortoise of North America (below) digs a tunnel 10 metres long to use as a home. During the warm days it emerges to feed on leaves.

The hawksbill turtle (below) is hunted for its attractive shell and therefore has become very rare.

The loggerhead turtle (right) lives in the warmer waters of the Pacific and Atlantic Oceans and hunts crabs and shellfish.

The leatherback turtle (below left) grows to 1.5 metres in length and is the largest turtle.

The map terrapin (below) lives in ponds in North America where it hunts crustaceans.

CHAMELEONS

Chameleons are truly the strangest of all lizards. There are many different species, no less than eighty-five in Africa and Madagascar, one in the Mediterranean countries and one in India.

The Mediterranean chameleons are about 30 centimetres in length. The giant chameleons of Madagascar, the largest of the species, measure a metre whereas the dwarf chameleons of South Africa measure only 11 centimetres.

They are amazing creatures for they can change their colouring at will through different shades of green, red, yellow and black. When enraged, chameleons will turn white. They can also alter the pattern of their colouring.

Chameleons have eyes that move independently but as can be seen in the above illustration, their eyes are completely covered (the term is "fused"). They can see very well though, for there is a small hole in each eyelid when their eyes are open. As their eyes move, so do the holes.

Their fingers and toes are fused, two on one side and three on the other. This enables them to climb very well in the trees and bushes where they make their homes.

There are sticky enlargements at the ends of their tongues. Should a chameleon catch sight of an insect, its long tongue darts out and the insect is caught, almost without exception, on the sticky tip. Then into the mouth of the chameleon goes the insect. The tongue is so long, it is longer than the chameleon's head and body.

Chapter Six
CRUSTACEANS

Crustaceans is the name given to a group of animals which includes lobsters, crabs, shrimps and barnacles.

There are many different groups. They are found all over the world, in fresh water, in the oceans and on land. They live in deserts and on mountain peaks. Most crustaceans, though, are creatures of the sea.

They range from big crabs and lobsters down to tiny animals that are difficult to see with the naked eye. The Japanese spider crab measures 3 metres across from leg-tip to leg-tip. The water flea is less than 0.5 of a millimetre.

Most crustaceans are good to eat.

CRABS

Nearly all crabs are water animals and breathe through gills in the same way as fish. Some swim on the surface of the sea, others crawl on the seabed while some live under rocks on the seashore.

Crabs have an upper shell, a pair of large pincer-claws, an abdomen, and four pairs of legs for walking, digging and sometimes swimming.

Above is a velvet swimming crab. It gets its name from the fine, velvety hair with which it is covered. It is quite common

around the coasts of Great Britain. Even though it is only a mere 10 centimetres across, the velvet swimming crab is known to be one of the fiercest crabs.

If it is disturbed by another crab, for instance, it will lash out with its pincer claws and fight furiously. It usually wins its battles.

There are about four thousand different types of crabs living in the oceans and, in a few cases, on land.

Some crabs are caught and sold as food. Of these the edible crab (above) is the best known. It is found off rocky coasts around Europe and is caught in large numbers. It feeds on dead fish and other decaying animal flesh. It grows to about 25 centimetres across.

Edible crabs are able to grow replacement legs and claws. If caught they will deliberately break off the trapped limb to escape. A new limb will develop over the next few months.

The hermit crab has no shell of its own. Its body is soft and vulnerable to attack. To protect itself it will crawl into an empty shell and in the illustration (left) a hermit crab is shown nestling in

the abandoned shell of a sea-snail. An odd feature is the anemone which has attached itself to the top of the shell. This occurs quite frequently.

The spider crab (above) takes its name from its long, slender legs. It is a master of disguise and often allows seaweed and sponges to grow on its back to help it blend in with its surroundings. The largest crab in the world is the Japanese spider crab which may have a shell 30 centimetres across and have legs 3.2 metres from tip to tip.

The shore crab (below) is unusual in that it is able to swim through the water as well as crawl on the seabed. It has powerful claws and will nip any intruder, even a human. The

shore crab can be found under boulders and in the cracks of rocks. It is either green or reddish-brown in colour.

The xantho crab lives in many areas of the tropics. It is a land crab and is unable to swim. An added drawback is that it cannot breathe under water. It therefore lives on sand dunes and above the level of the high tide. When danger threatens it can scamper to safety across the dunes very quickly.

LOBSTERS

Lobsters, shrimps and prawns all belong to the same family. Lobsters have four pairs of legs and strong, grasping claws.

The common lobster is found around European coasts and grows to about 50 centimetres in length. It is a scavenger, and eats dead fish and other animals.

The squat lobster (below) has long antennae (or feelers) growing from its head. It is seen more often in water than on shore.

Both crabs and lobsters hatch from eggs. The eggs may take six months to hatch. The young take as long as three or four years to become fully grown.

The crawfish (below) is bigger than the common lobster but has smaller claws.

It is a marine creature which lives near coasts and often comes ashore in search of food.

On each of its long feelers there are rough surfaces which it can rub together to make a noise that frightens away its enemies.

They make very popular meals.

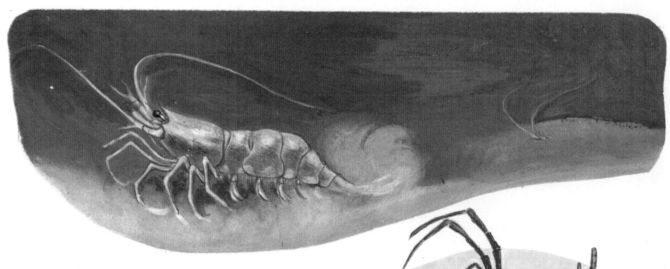

The shrimp (above) is a very good swimmer. It swims backwards using its legs, which are called swimmerets, and by quick strokes of its tail. The common sand shrimp is often found on the seashore where there is shallow water with a sandy bottom. When it is frightened, it buries itself in the sand until only its long feelers can be seen.

Some shrimps trick their enemies by changing the colour of their bodies to match their surroundings. The tropical skeleton shrimp (right) for example, not only copies the colour but also the shape of the seaweed on which it feeds.

In appearance, prawns (below) are rather like shrimps but there is an obvious difference. The prawn is twice the size of a shrimp and its head has a kind of beak with teeth like those on a saw. Also the prawn is greenish-grey in colour and the first two pairs of its legs have pincers like those of a crab.

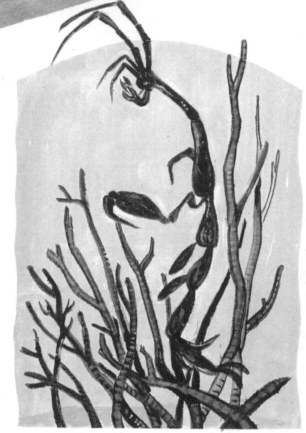

Like crabs and lobsters, prawns and shrimps often appear on restaurant menus all over the world.

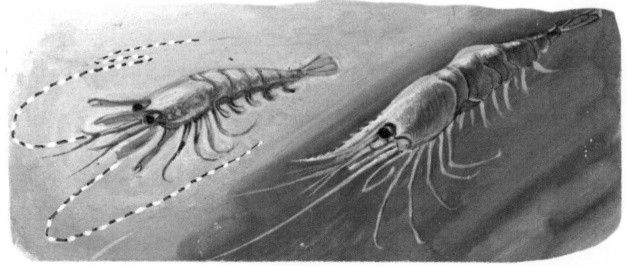

INDEX